Lord, Teach Us to Pray

How to Have a Daily Quiet Time Alone with God

REV. JOHN S. MAHON

WESTBOW°
PRESS
A DIVISION OF THOMAS NELSON
& ZONDERVAN

WestBow Press books may be ordered through booksellers or by contacting:

WestBow Press
A Division of Thomas Nelson & Zondervan
1663 Liberty Drive
Bloomington, IN 47403
www.westbowpress.com
1 (866) 928-1240

ISBN: 978-1-4908-6913-1 (sc)
ISBN: 978-1-4908-6914-8 (e)

Library of Congress Control Number: 2015902107

Print information available on the last page.

WestBow Press rev. date: 03/12/2015

Dedication

This workbook is dedicated to Sam Clark—missionary, friend, spiritual mentor, and godfather to my son (after whom he is named). By this faithful man's guidance and influence, I became convinced of the practice of the daily quiet time alone with God.

CONTENTS

Moving Forward

Appendix

PREFACE

This workbook is designed to aid the follower of Christ's growth through the introduction of a daily quiet time alone with God. Beginning with the simple disciplines of prayer and meditation upon God's Word, this workbook prepares disciples to develop their own prayer notebooks based upon a deeper dependence upon God and understanding of His character as it relates to prayer. I am convinced that laying the foundation for discipleship begins with practicing the daily quiet time alone with God. In my experience, although only about one in ten individuals involved in Bible study go on to be disciple-makers, a full 50 percent of persons who give themselves to the discipline of the daily quiet time alone with God fulfill Christ's calling to go and make disciples.

Consequently, I hope that in mastering this discipline of time alone with God, you experience not only growth as a disciple but become equipped with a skill by which you commit to disciple others. Not everyone has the gift of teaching; not everyone has the gift of leadership; not everyone has been called to pastor a church; but everyone can disciple another Christian.

The daily quiet time alone with God serves as the beginning of this discipleship process. I leave this workbook with you with the solemn exhortation that I penned these words, not solely for your benefit, but also for the benefit of that man or woman whom you begin to disciple through the discipline of the daily quiet time alone with God.

By His mercy,
Rev. John S. Mahon
2 Corinthians 4:1
Director, Grace Community International
January 2015

ACKNOWLEDGMENTS

The *Lord, Teach Us to Pray* workbook has undergone many revisions over the years. A special thanks to Charles Casebolt, Navigator representative at the University of Texas at Austin, who first taught me the philosophy of personal discipleship. Additionally, I am indebted to Navigator missionary and statesman, John Crawford, for the motivation and encouragement to put my ideas down in workbook form so that others might learn how to pray by using the simple and practical disciplines taught in the Word of God. My wife, Eleanor, served as the first editor and typist of this workbook long before the age of computers. Later, my faithful secretary, Patsy Carver Starks, spent many hours typing, editing, and patiently applying my revisions. My good friend, Dr. John Mertz, read through this workbook several times, making recommendations to ensure the workbook acted as a stand-alone volume. Finally, my daughter, Liz Izaguirre, MPH, and her husband, Rev. José Izaguirre, ThM, provided much valuable input. Liz spent many hours editing and painfully aiding me in improvements for the development of this final edition.

This workbook is a labor of love. I had my first quiet time alone with God in 1970 after being taught how to do so one-on-one by a Navigator disciple-maker. I attended my first Navigator workshop entitled *How to Pray* in 1971 taught by Ken Choate, missionary to China. I was encouraged to go deeper in prayer by missionary Sam Clark. I have taught this workbook in twenty-seven countries, and this work has been translated into a number of languages. At each stage along the way, countless suggestions were made concerning its improvement. Time and space do not allow for acknowledgment of all of the spiritual and personal help that I have received over the years. However, it is my hope that this volume will assist you, the reader, in answering your prayer, *Lord, teach me to pray.*

Starting the Journey

CHAPTER 1

Introduction to the Daily Quiet Time Alone with God

In the early morning, while it was still dark, Jesus got up, left the house, and went away to a secluded place, and was praying there.

—Mark 1:35

Sweet hour of prayer, sweet hour of prayer,
Thy wings shall my petition bear
To Him whose truth and faithfulness
Engage the waiting soul to bless:
And since He bids me seek His face,
Believe His Word, and trust His grace,
I'll cast on Him my every care
And wait for thee, sweet hour of prayer.

—*Sweet Hour of Prayer*

Has there ever been an opportunity in your life on which you later look back and think *I wish I had taken that more seriously?* Have you ever spent time alone with someone you love? Do you remember how important were those fleeting, precious times all to yourselves? Now consider the prospect of spending quiet time alone with God on a daily basis. What an opportunity of a lifetime! Because of our new relationship with God through faith in Jesus Christ, such communion can be a daily reality. This workbook strives to aid the disciple of Jesus Christ in fully utilizing these times alone with God.

Getting Started

To begin this exciting new facet of your relationship with God, four simple items are necessary: a pen, a Bible, a quiet spot (where you can think and pray), and the *Lord, Teach Us to Pray* workbook.

Scripture overflows with examples of individuals who practiced this art of spending quiet time alone with God. Read Mark 1:35 and Psalm 119:147–148. Record in the space below what characterized the quiet times alone with God of both Jesus and David.

Having Your Own Time with God

The exciting thing about spending quiet time alone with God is that He is always present with us. When we pray, we pray in the presence of God. When we read the Bible, God is with us, speaking to us. We do not have to go to a church, a preacher, a priest, or a special location to communicate with God. Nor do we need a special posture, to close our eyes, fold our hands, or bow our heads. In having daily quiet times alone with God, He simply asks us to come to Him. However, we may choose the surroundings, methods, or styles that prove the most comfortable to us.

How do the following verses reflect the truth that when we practice quiet time alone with God, we rest in His very presence?

- Hebrews 4:16
- Hebrews 10:19–20
- James 4:8

Choose a verse with an especially meaningful message to you from this study. Now go to the front cover of the workbook and write this passage out. When satan tempts you to doubt the value of your daily quiet time alone with God, this passage will bolster and encourage you to persevere in this discipline.

Now all that is left for you to do is to turn the page and get started. Do not be threatened or dismayed by the brevity of the instructions for each day's quiet time. These directions were purposely written in this way because these hours are *your* quiet times alone with God. You will develop your own style of communicating with God and of hearing Him speak to you. Do not worry about doing the quiet time *wrong*. Simply complete each step before moving on to the next section. Remember, God loves you and is very excited about the prospect of spending focused time alone with you.

Relax, and enjoy your Creator, Savior, and heavenly Father.

Quiet Times for Weeks
One and Two

Date: _____   Passage: Joshua 1:7–8

  ⇒ **Request** that God speak to you from His Word.
  ⇒ **Read** the passage.
  ⇒ **Record** in the space below what God said.

  ⇒ **Reflect** on how this will affect your life today.

_____

Date: _____   Passage: Psalm 19:7–14

  ⇒ **Request** that God speak to you from His Word.
  ⇒ **Read** the passage.
  ⇒ **Record** in the space below what God said.

  ⇒ **Reflect** on how this will affect your life today.

Date: _____   Passage: Psalm 27:4

⇒ **Request** that God speak to you from His Word.
⇒ **Read** the passage.
⇒ **Record** in the space below what God said.

⇒ **Reflect** on how this will affect your life today.

Date: _____   Passage: Psalm 77:11–15

⇒ **Request** that God speak to you from His Word.
⇒ **Read** the passage.
⇒ **Record** in the space below what God said.

⇒ **Reflect** on how this will affect your life today.

Date: _____   Passage: Psalm 86:10–12

⇒ **Request** that God speak to you from His Word.
⇒ **Read** the passage.
⇒ **Record** in the space below what God said.

⇒ **Reflect** on how this will affect your life today.

_____

Date: _____   Passage: Psalm 119:12–16

⇒ **Request** that God speak to you from His Word.
⇒ **Read** the passage.
⇒ **Record** in the space below what God said.

⇒ **Reflect** on how this will affect your life today.

Date: _____   Passage: Psalm 119:17–19

⇒ **Request** that God speak to you from His Word.
⇒ **Read** the passage.
⇒ **Record** in the space below what God said.

⇒ **Reflect** on how this will affect your life today.

Date: _____   Passage: Psalm 119:25–32

⇒ **Request** that God speak to you from His Word.
⇒ **Read** the passage.
⇒ **Record** in the space below what God said.

⇒ **Reflect** on how this will affect your life today.

Date: _____   Passage: Psalm 119:44–48

⇒ **Request** that God speak to you from His Word.
⇒ **Read** the passage.
⇒ **Record** in the space below what God said.

⇒ **Reflect** on how this will affect your life today.

Date: _____   Passage: Psalm 119:49–56

⇒ **Request** that God speak to you from His Word.
⇒ **Read** the passage.
⇒ **Record** in the space below what God said.

⇒ **Reflect** on how this will affect your life today.

Date: _____   Passage: Psalm 119:97–104

   ⇒ **Request** that God speak to you from His Word.
   ⇒ **Read** the passage.
   ⇒ **Record** in the space below what God said.

   ⇒ **Reflect** on how this will affect your life today.

Date: _____   Passage: Psalm 119:145–148

   ⇒ **Request** that God speak to you from His Word.
   ⇒ **Read** the passage.
   ⇒ **Record** in the space below what God said.

   ⇒ **Reflect** on how this will affect your life today.

Date: _____   Passage: Psalm 143:5–8

⇒ **Request** that God speak to you from His Word.
⇒ **Read** the passage.
⇒ **Record** in the space below what God said.

⇒ **Reflect** on how this will affect your life today.

Date: _____   Passage: Psalm 145:1–5

⇒ **Request** that God speak to you from His Word.
⇒ **Read** the passage.
⇒ **Record** in the space below what God said.

⇒ **Reflect** on how this will affect your life today.

CHAPTER 2

How to Pray

It happened that while Jesus was praying in a certain place,
after He had finished, one of His disciples said to Him,
"Lord, teach us to pray just as John also taught his disciples."

—Luke 11:1

What a Friend we have in Jesus, all our sins and griefs to bear!
What a privilege to carry everything to God in prayer!
O, what peace we often forfeit, O, what needless pain we bear,
All because we do not carry everything to God in prayer!

—*What a Friend We Have in Jesus*

Have you ever experienced a situation in which if you had understood everything at the beginning as you understood things at the end, you would have acted and spoken differently? All of us are continually growing in our ability to communicate. When it comes to our relationship with God, saying the *right thing* is not as important as growing in our understanding of the options and opportunities for communication with Him that He opens to us.

You have now been meeting with God for personal quiet times for two weeks and should be getting comfortable with God and with recognizing His voice as He speaks to you from His Word. It is only natural at this time that you should begin to desire to know God more. What are the avenues? What has God revealed to us to help us communicate with Him? How can we know Him more intimately, and how can we use our time alone with Him most effectively? In other words, how can we grow in our relationship with Him?

Putting Away the Child

Up to this point, you have been relating to God as a child. In your relationship with God, you may be experiencing the same frustration that a child knows in finding it difficult to express himself to his loving Father. This next section focuses on equipping you to communicate well with God. Read 1 Corinthians 13:11, and write in the space below what your attitude ought to be as you mature in your relationship with God.

Friendship with Christ

Starting now, determine in your heart to begin to do away with childish things as they pertain to prayer. Now is the time for you to learn to interact with God as an adult and as His friend, rather than just as His child. Read John 15:15, and reflect in the space provided what this passage communicates regarding the changed status of our relationship with God in Christ.

Six Disciplines of Prayer

You now possess the privilege of speaking to God as His friend. In return, He also converses with you as a friend (though you will always be His child), revealing more of His person, love, and will.

The following section discusses in detail six disciplines of prayer that the friend of God utilizes in communicating with Him:

- How to *praise* God,
- How to *confess* our sins to God,
- How to *thank* God,
- How to present *our needs* to God,
- How to present the *needs of others* to God, and
- How to engage in *spiritual warfare*.

In Luke 11:1 what do the disciples ask Jesus to do for them?

Before beginning this next section, I suggest that you spend some time with God, your Creator, your Savior, and yes, your Friend. In the space below, write out a short prayer asking Him to teach you to pray.

SPIRITUAL
DISCIPLINES
OF PRAYER

CHAPTER 3

Adoration

Praise the Lord! For it is good to sing praises to our God;
For it is pleasant and praise is becoming.

—Psalm 147:1

Holy, holy, holy! Lord God Almighty!
Early in the morning our song shall rise to Thee.
Holy, holy, holy! Merciful and Mighty!
God in three Persons, blessed Trinity!

—*Holy, Holy, Holy! Lord God Almighty*

Can you imagine having a relationship with someone who possessed only two thoughts: *What have you fixed me to eat?* followed by *Now here is a list of things I want you do for me?* Have you ever had someone ask to speak with you privately, only to find out that they wanted something *from* you rather than wanted to spend time *with* you? Up until now, your prayers to God focused on His giving you knowledge and feeding you from His Word. Yet our relationship with God ought to consist of more than simple cries of *Give me! Give me! Give me!*

Maturing Your Relationship with God

We anticipate this type of behavior from a child. Small children pretty much live at this psychosocial level all of the time, and we expect them to do so. But as the child matures into a young person, such behavior becomes less and less *cute*. Parents especially begin to expect the young adult to express some sort of appreciation and gratitude. In the space below, reflect on how you would characterize your interaction with God, specifically in terms of content. Are your conversations with Him those of a child or a mature adult?

Now turn in your Bible to the following passages and read them carefully. Next to each verse, write a key word or phrase that you feel sums up what is taking place.

- Psalm 100:4
- Psalm 146:1–2
- Psalm 147:1
- Psalm 149:1–4
- Psalm 150:1–6
- Hebrews 13:15–16

Notice how all of the above passages refer to the importance of the adoration of God. Reflecting on these passages, choose a verse that best expresses your feelings in this area, and circle the verse. Now turn to the Convictions in Prayer page of this workbook (page 105). Under *Type of Prayer* and *Scripture Reference* in space number one, write *Adoration* followed by the previously selected verse that spoke the most clearly to you on this issue. Then in the space provided underneath these headings, write out the verse in its entirety. Now when satan tempts you not to praise God, you possess an answer for satan from Scripture.

Adoration v. Thanksgiving

As a result of this new conviction and before you ask God to speak to you in your quiet times, you will spend time praising Him. However, it is important to understand the difference between praising God and thanking Him. Adoration involves the worship of the person of God *without* reference to man. On the other hand, thanksgiving consists of the expression of appreciation to God for His actions towards man. Read the following prayers, and indicate which statement expresses adoration and which prayer offers thanksgiving.

- "O Lord, I worship You as the one and only true God. You are a God of power and might, and I worship You for who and what You are. You are the only true Lord and God of heaven and earth, all powerful and sovereign."
  - Type of prayer:

- "O Lord, I appreciate so much how You sovereignly watch over me. Your power and strength are continually helping me in my daily life. As God of heaven and earth, You provide for all of my needs. What a blessing to me You are!"
  - Type of prayer:

These next two weeks of quiet times alone with God focus on adoration as an important component of offering prayers to God. Remember to check off the appropriate diamond next to each discipline of prayer as you complete it during your daily quiet time with God.

Quiet Times for Weeks Three and Four

Date: _____   Passage: Psalm 30:1–12

> ⇒ **Remember** the disciplines of prayer (◊ praise).
> ⇒ **Request** that God speak to you from His Word.
> ⇒ **Read** the passage.
> ⇒ **Record** in the space below what God said.

> ⇒ **Reflect** on how this will affect your life today.

Date: _____   Passage: Psalm 67:1–7

> ⇒ **Remember** the disciplines of prayer (◊ praise).
> ⇒ **Request** that God speak to you from His Word.
> ⇒ **Read** the passage.
> ⇒ **Record** in the space below what God said.

> ⇒ **Reflect** on how this will affect your life today.

Date: _____   Passage: Psalm 95:1–7

⇒ **Remember** the disciplines of prayer (◊ praise).
⇒ **Request** that God speak to you from His Word.
⇒ **Read** the passage.
⇒ **Record** in the space below what God said.

⇒ **Reflect** on how this will affect your life today.

Date: _____   Passage: Psalm 99:1–9

⇒ **Remember** the disciplines of prayer (◊ praise).
⇒ **Request** that God speak to you from His Word.
⇒ **Read** the passage.
⇒ **Record** in the space below what God said.

⇒ **Reflect** on how this will affect your life today.

Date: _____   Passage: Psalm 100:1–5

   ⇒ **Remember** the disciplines of prayer (◊ praise).
   ⇒ **Request** that God speak to you from His Word.
   ⇒ **Read** the passage.
   ⇒ **Record** in the space below what God said.

   ⇒ **Reflect** on how this will affect your life today.

Date: _____   Passage: Psalm 111:1–10

   ⇒ **Remember** the disciplines of prayer (◊ praise).
   ⇒ **Request** that God speak to you from His Word.
   ⇒ **Read** the passage.
   ⇒ **Record** in the space below what God said.

   ⇒ **Reflect** on how this will affect your life today.

Date: _____   Passage: Psalm 139:1–12

⇒ **Remember** the disciplines of prayer (◊ praise).
⇒ **Request** that God speak to you from His Word.
⇒ **Read** the passage.
⇒ **Record** in the space below what God said.

⇒ **Reflect** on how this will affect your life today.

Date: _____   Passage: Psalm 139:13–24

⇒ **Remember** the disciplines of prayer (◊ praise).
⇒ **Request** that God speak to you from His Word.
⇒ **Read** the passage.
⇒ **Record** in the space below what God said.

⇒ **Reflect** on how this will affect your life today.

Date: _____   Passage: Psalm 145:1–24

   ⇒ **Remember** the disciplines of prayer (◊ praise).
   ⇒ **Request** that God speak to you from His Word.
   ⇒ **Read** the passage.
   ⇒ **Record** in the space below what God said.

   ⇒ **Reflect** on how this will affect your life today.

Date: _____   Passage: Psalm 146:1–10

   ⇒ **Remember** the disciplines of prayer (◊ praise).
   ⇒ **Request** that God speak to you from His Word.
   ⇒ **Read** the passage.
   ⇒ **Record** in the space below what God said.

   ⇒ **Reflect** on how this will affect your life today.

Date: _____   Passage: Psalm 147:1–20

   ⇒ **Remember** the disciplines of prayer (◊ praise).
   ⇒ **Request** that God speak to you from His Word.
   ⇒ **Read** the passage.
   ⇒ **Record** in the space below what God said.

   ⇒ **Reflect** on how this will affect your life today.

Date: _____   Passage: Psalm 148:1–14

   ⇒ **Remember** the disciplines of prayer (◊ praise).
   ⇒ **Request** that God speak to you from His Word.
   ⇒ **Read** the passage.
   ⇒ **Record** in the space below what God said.

   ⇒ **Reflect** on how this will affect your life today.

Date: _____   Passage: Psalm 149:1–9

   ⇒ **Remember** the disciplines of prayer (◊ praise).
   ⇒ **Request** that God speak to you from His Word.
   ⇒ **Read** the passage.
   ⇒ **Record** in the space below what God said.

   ⇒ **Reflect** on how this will affect your life today.

Date: _____   Passage: Psalm 150:1–6

   ⇒ **Remember** the disciplines of prayer (◊ praise).
   ⇒ **Request** that God speak to you from His Word.
   ⇒ **Read** the passage.
   ⇒ **Record** in the space below what God said.

   ⇒ **Reflect** on how this will affect your life today.

CHAPTER 4

Confession

I acknowledged my sin to You, and my iniquity I did not hide;
I said, "I will confess my transgressions to the Lord;"
and You forgave the guilt of my sin. Selah.

—Psalm 32:5

Let me at the throne of mercy find a sweet relief;
Kneeling there in deep contrition, help my unbelief.
Savior, Savior, hear my humble cry;
While on others Thou art calling, do not pass me by.

—Pass Me Not

Until now the issue that brought you to Christ in the first place—sin—has not been addressed. Since becoming a Christian, you may have developed a painful awareness that you continue to sin. Despite your best efforts this battle with the flesh continues and affects your relationship with God.

Sin and the Believer

Two questions move in the heart of any believer struggling with the reality of sin, despite the assured redemption of Christ. In the space provided below, write out the scriptural response to each of these questions.

- Question: Will I ever get to the point where I stop sinning?
  - Answer: 1 John 1:8–10

- Question: When I sin, does that mean that I will lose my salvation?
  - Answer: Romans 8:1, 38–39

The Importance of Confession

The answers to the above two questions beg a third one. If it is true that you will never cease to sin, and it is equally true that your sin will never cause you to lose your salvation, then what good is confession? Why bother with confessing sin at all? The answer to this critical question consists of two parts.

First, God is a personal God such that when you sin, your sin affects your interpersonal relationship with Him. According to Ephesians 4:30, our sin hurts God and causes Him grief. Just as in any close relationship with another individual, to admit one's faults and to ask for forgiveness serves to forge a deeper connection. Confession then does not affect God's relationship with us, but this act deeply impacts our relationship with God.

Secondly, God teaches us to confess our sins in His Word. Read Luke 11:1–4. What specific instruction does Jesus provide His disciples regarding prayer?

Next, look up the following passages in your Bible, and read them carefully. Across from each reference, write a word or phrase to sum up the heart or main message of the passage.

- Psalm 41:4
- Psalm 66:18
- Psalm 79:9
- Isaiah 59:1–2
- Micah 3:4
- Luke 18:13
- 1 John 1:9

Notice that all of the above passages refer to confessing your sins to God. Reflecting on these passages, choose a verse that best expresses your feelings in this area, and circle the verse. Now turn to the Convictions in Prayer page of this workbook (page 105). Under *Type of Prayer* and *Scripture Reference* in space number two, write *Confession* followed by the previously selected verse that spoke the most clearly to you on this issue. Then in the space provided underneath these headings, write out the verse in its entirety. Now when satan tempts you to not confess your sins to God, you possess an answer for him.

Now it is time to continue your growth as a disciple in prayer. Remember, before you ask God to speak to and feed you from His Word, you will want to praise God and then confess your sins. Check off the appropriate diamond next to each discipline of prayer as you complete it during your daily quiet time with God. Only after you complete these two components of mature prayer will you ask God to speak to you from His Word.

QUIET TIMES FOR WEEKS FIVE AND SIX

Date: _____   Passage: Psalm 25:1–7

⇒ **Remember** the disciplines of prayer (◊ praise, ◊ confession).
⇒ **Request** that God speak to you from His Word.
⇒ **Read** the passage.
⇒ **Record** in the space below what God said.

⇒ **Reflect** on how this will affect your life today.

_____

Date: _____   Passage: Psalm 39:1–13

⇒ **Remember** the disciplines of prayer (◊ praise, ◊ confession).
⇒ **Request** that God speak to you from His Word.
⇒ **Read** the passage.
⇒ **Record** in the space below what God said.

⇒ **Reflect** on how this will affect your life today.

Date: _____   Passage: Psalm 40:1–17

    ⇒ **Remember** the disciplines of prayer (◊ praise, ◊ confession).
    ⇒ **Request** that God speak to you from His Word.
    ⇒ **Read** the passage.
    ⇒ **Record** in the space below what God said.

    ⇒ **Reflect** on how this will affect your life today.

Date: _____   Passage: Psalm 41:1–13

    ⇒ **Remember** the disciplines of prayer (◊ praise, ◊ confession).
    ⇒ **Request** that God speak to you from His Word.
    ⇒ **Read** the passage.
    ⇒ **Record** in the space below what God said.

    ⇒ **Reflect** on how this will affect your life today.

Date: _____   Passage: Psalm 51:1–19

    ⇒ **Remember** the disciplines of prayer (◊ praise, ◊ confession).
    ⇒ **Request** that God speak to you from His Word.
    ⇒ **Read** the passage.
    ⇒ **Record** in the space below what God said.

    ⇒ **Reflect** on how this will affect your life today.

Date: _____   Passage: Psalm 65:1–13

    ⇒ **Remember** the disciplines of prayer (◊ praise, ◊ confession).
    ⇒ **Request** that God speak to you from His Word.
    ⇒ **Read** the passage.
    ⇒ **Record** in the space below what God said.

    ⇒ **Reflect** on how this will affect your life today.

Date: _____   Passage: Psalm 79:1–13

⇒ **Remember** the disciplines of prayer (◊ praise, ◊ confession).
⇒ **Request** that God speak to you from His Word.
⇒ **Read** the passage.
⇒ **Record** in the space below what God said.

⇒ **Reflect** on how this will affect your life today.

Date: _____   Passage: Psalm 80:1–19

⇒ **Remember** the disciplines of prayer (◊ praise, ◊ confession).
⇒ **Request** that God speak to you from His Word.
⇒ **Read** the passage.
⇒ **Record** in the space below what God said.

⇒ **Reflect** on how this will affect your life today.

Date: _____   Passage: Psalm 103:1–22

⇒ **Remember** the disciplines of prayer (◊ praise, ◊ confession).
⇒ **Request** that God speak to you from His Word.
⇒ **Read** the passage.
⇒ **Record** in the space below what God said.

⇒ **Reflect** on how this will affect your life today.

Date: _____   Passage: Isaiah 59:1–3

⇒ **Remember** the disciplines of prayer (◊ praise, ◊ confession).
⇒ **Request** that God speak to you from His Word.
⇒ **Read** the passage.
⇒ **Record** in the space below what God said.

⇒ **Reflect** on how this will affect your life today.

Date: _____   Passage: Luke 11:1–4

⇒ **Remember** the disciplines of prayer (◊ praise, ◊ confession).
⇒ **Request** that God speak to you from His Word.
⇒ **Read** the passage.
⇒ **Record** in the space below what God said.

⇒ **Reflect** on how this will affect your life today.

Date: _____   Passage: Luke 18:9–14

⇒ **Remember** the disciplines of prayer (◊ praise, ◊ confession).
⇒ **Request** that God speak to you from His Word.
⇒ **Read** the passage.
⇒ **Record** in the space below what God said.

⇒ **Reflect** on how this will affect your life today.

Date: _____   Passage: Romans 10:8–13

    ⇒ **Remember** the disciplines of prayer (◊ praise, ◊ confession).
    ⇒ **Request** that God speak to you from His Word.
    ⇒ **Read** the passage.
    ⇒ **Record** in the space below what God said.

    ⇒ **Reflect** on how this will affect your life today.

Date: _____   Passage: 1 John 1:8–10

    ⇒ **Remember** the disciplines of prayer (◊ praise, ◊ confession).
    ⇒ **Request** that God speak to you from His Word.
    ⇒ **Read** the passage.
    ⇒ **Record** in the space below what God said.

    ⇒ **Reflect** on how this will affect your life today.

Chapter 5

Thanksgiving

Rejoice always; pray without ceasing;
in everything give thanks; for this is God's will for
you in Christ Jesus.

—1 Thessalonians 5:16–18

Frail children of dust, and feeble as frail,
In Thee do we trust, nor find Thee to fail.
Thy mercies how tender, how firm to the end!
Our Maker, Defender, Redeemer, and Friend!

—O Worship the King

Remember the last time you did something sacrificial that you thought went unnoticed until someone later came up and thanked you for it? How did that one expression of thankfulness make you feel about that person? Now consider the other side of the coin. What happens in the life of the thankful person in terms of his or her character? What is the importance of children thanking their parents? Certainly this does not decide whether or not their parents love them or keep them.

The Importance of Thankfulness

In your quiet times alone with God, you must not forget the importance of a word of thanks in developing a close interpersonal relationship with Him, as well as in the development of your own spiritual character. Turn now in your Bible to the following passages, and make a note next to each reference how the passage describes the practice of giving thanks to God.

- Psalm 92:1–2
- Psalm 100:1–5
- Psalm 118:1, 29
- Psalm 136:1–3, 26
- Psalm 138:1–2
- Luke 17:11–19
- Hebrews 13:15–16

Developing a Thankful Lifestyle

As you reflect back on your own life, consider the relationships listed below. Thinking about these relationships, which do you generally do more of—ask for specific things or offer thanks for specific things? Draw a circle around any type of relationship in which you thank the person more than ask them for something. Conversely, draw a box around any type of relationship in which you ask the person for something more often than thank the individual.

Spouse	Family	Ministers
Coworkers	Friends	God

Consider the ratio of circles to boxes above. In your interpersonal relationships, are you more likely to ask people for something or to thank them?

Reflecting on the above passages, choose a verse that best expresses your feelings in this area, and circle the verse. Now turn to the Convictions in Prayer page of this workbook (page 105). Under *Type of Prayer* and *Scripture Reference* in space number three, write *Thanksgiving* followed by the previously selected verse that spoke the most clearly to you on this issue. Then in the space provided underneath these headings, write out the verse in its entirety. Now when satan tempts you to not thank God, you possess an answer with which to rebuke him. Additionally, if your own sinful self is in the habit of not thanking others (much less God), you have a reminder of this important practice.

Now you are ready to continue on in your daily quiet times with God, adding the discipline of thanksgiving to your prayers. As you pray, begin with praising God, then confess your sins to God. Prior to asking Him for anything, express your appreciation by giving Him the thanks He so richly deserves. Check off the appropriate diamond next to each discipline of prayer as you complete it during your daily quiet time with God. By adopting these practices, you will resemble the leper who gave thanks in Luke, chapter 17 and not the other nine lepers who failed to turn back.

Quiet Times for Weeks Seven and Eight

Date: _____   Passage: Deuteronomy 28:47–48

⇒ **Remember** the disciplines of prayer (◊ praise, ◊ confession, ◊ thanksgiving).
⇒ **Request** that God speak to you from His Word.
⇒ **Read** the passage.
⇒ **Record** in the space below what God said.

⇒ **Reflect** on how this will affect your life today.

_____

Date: _____   Passage: Psalm 50:23

⇒ **Remember** the disciplines of prayer (◊ praise, ◊ confession, ◊ thanksgiving).
⇒ **Request** that God speak to you from His Word.
⇒ **Read** the passage.
⇒ **Record** in the space below what God said.

⇒ **Reflect** on how this will affect your life today.

Date: _____   Passage: Psalm 92:1–4

⇒ **Remember** the disciplines of prayer (◊ praise, ◊ confession, ◊ thanksgiving).
⇒ **Request** that God speak to you from His Word.
⇒ **Read** the passage.
⇒ **Record** in the space below what God said.

⇒ **Reflect** on how this will affect your life today.

_____

Date: _____   Passage: Psalm 100:1–5

⇒ **Remember** the disciplines of prayer (◊ praise, ◊ confession, ◊ thanksgiving).
⇒ **Request** that God speak to you from His Word.
⇒ **Read** the passage.
⇒ **Record** in the space below what God said.

⇒ **Reflect** on how this will affect your life today.

Date: _____   Passage: Psalm 107:1–9, 42–43

  ⇒ **Remember** the disciplines of prayer (◊ praise, ◊ confession, ◊ thanksgiving).
  ⇒ **Request** that God speak to you from His Word.
  ⇒ **Read** the passage.
  ⇒ **Record** in the space below what God said.

  ⇒ **Reflect** on how this will affect your life today.

Date: _____   Passage: Psalm 118:1–2, 28–29

  ⇒ **Remember** the disciplines of prayer (◊ praise, ◊ confession, ◊ thanksgiving).
  ⇒ **Request** that God speak to you from His Word.
  ⇒ **Read** the passage.
  ⇒ **Record** in the space below what God said.

  ⇒ **Reflect** on how this will affect your life today.

Date: _____ Passage: Psalm 136:1–26

⇒ **Remember** the disciplines of prayer (◊ praise, ◊ confession, ◊ thanksgiving).
⇒ **Request** that God speak to you from His Word.
⇒ **Read** the passage.
⇒ **Record** in the space below what God said.

⇒ **Reflect** on how this will affect your life today.

Date: _____ Passage: Psalm 138:1–8

⇒ **Remember** the disciplines of prayer (◊ praise, ◊ confession, ◊ thanksgiving).
⇒ **Request** that God speak to you from His Word.
⇒ **Read** the passage.
⇒ **Record** in the space below what God said.

⇒ **Reflect** on how this will affect your life today.

Date: _____   Passage: Psalm 140:12–13

⇒ **Remember** the disciplines of prayer (◊ praise, ◊ confession, ◊ thanksgiving).
⇒ **Request** that God speak to you from His Word.
⇒ **Read** the passage.
⇒ **Record** in the space below what God said.

⇒ **Reflect** on how this will affect your life today.

Date: _____   Passage: Philippians 4:6–7

⇒ **Remember** the disciplines of prayer (◊ praise, ◊ confession, ◊ thanksgiving).
⇒ **Request** that God speak to you from His Word.
⇒ **Read** the passage.
⇒ **Record** in the space below what God said.

⇒ **Reflect** on how this will affect your life today.

Date: _____   Passage: Colossians 3:15–16, 4:2

⇒ **Remember** the disciplines of prayer (◊ praise, ◊ confession, ◊ thanksgiving).
⇒ **Request** that God speak to you from His Word.
⇒ **Read** the passage.
⇒ **Record** in the space below what God said.

⇒ **Reflect** on how this will affect your life today.

Date: _____   Passage: 1 Thessalonians 5:16–18

⇒ **Remember** the disciplines of prayer (◊ praise, ◊ confession, ◊ thanksgiving).
⇒ **Request** that God speak to you from His Word.
⇒ **Read** the passage.
⇒ **Record** in the space below what God said.

⇒ **Reflect** on how this will affect your life today.

Date: _____   Passage: 2 Thessalonians 1:3–4

⇒ **Remember** the disciplines of prayer (◊ praise, ◊ confession, ◊ thanksgiving).
⇒ **Request** that God speak to you from His Word.
⇒ **Read** the passage.
⇒ **Record** in the space below what God.

⇒ **Reflect** on how this will affect your life today.

Date: _____   Passage: Hebrews 13:15–16

⇒ **Remember** the disciplines of prayer (◊ praise, ◊ confession, ◊ thanksgiving).
⇒ **Request** that God speak to you from His Word.
⇒ **Read** the passage.
⇒ **Record** in the space below what God said.

⇒ **Reflect** on how this will affect your life today.

CHAPTER 6

Supplication

This is the confidence which we have before Him,
that, if we ask anything according to His will, He hears us.
And if we know that He hears us in whatever we ask,
we know that we have the requests which we have asked from Him.

—1 John 5:14–15

More love to Thee, O Christ, more love to Thee!
Hear Thou the prayer I make on bended knee.
This is my earnest plea: More love, O Christ, to Thee;
More love to Thee, more love to Thee!

—*More Love to Thee*

Have you ever been asked for something by a person you knew was nervous about the request—wondering if they were asking for too much—when for you it was no big deal? Have you ever had to turn down someone's request because you felt that granting the request was not in the person's best interest?

When you think about making requests to God, you need to remember His status as your Father and Friend. He desires for you to come to Him with your requests; indeed, it brings Him great delight when you bring your petitions before Him. After all, He feels free to ask things of you, and He wants you as His friend to feel the same welcome in His presence. Unlike you, though, God possesses the freedom to turn you down based on His infinite knowledge of what is best for you. What kind of relationship would you have with an individual if, when presented with a request for which his reply was no, your response was, *Well, you're no true friend of mine.* Or what if your spouse doubted the validity of your marriage any time you turned down a request?

The Petitioner's Attitude

Thus far in this workbook, you have asked God for things based on your feeding upon His Word and His speaking to you about an issue from His Word. In the space below describe the assurance given in 1 John 5:14–15 concerning this approach to asking God for things.

James 4:3–4 provides a description of the more conventional *Give me! Give me! Give me!* approach to making supplications to God. Read this passage, and answer the following questions.

- Which of these two approaches better resembles your prayers, 1 John 5:14–15 or James 4:3–4?

- Why do you suppose that this is true of your prayer life?

- Have you ever felt like many of your prayers go unanswered? How might these verses shed some light on that dilemma? Explain.

Presenting Your Requests

Turn in your Bible to the verses listed below. As you read through them note how each of these passages refers to asking God for things.

- Psalm 116:1–2
- Isaiah 62:6–7
- Philippians 4:6–7, 19–20
- John 16:23–24
- James 4:1–5

Reflecting on these passages, choose a verse that best expresses your feelings in this area, and circle the verse. Now turn to the Convictions in Prayer page of this workbook (page 105). Under *Type of Prayer* and *Scripture Reference* in space number four, write *Supplication* followed by the previously selected verse that spoke the most clearly to you on this issue. Then in the space provided underneath these headings, write out the verse in its entirety. Now when satan challenges you when you ask God for something, you possess an answer with which to rebuke him.

Before continuing on to the next section containing quiet times for weeks nine and ten, complete the two worksheets located in the back of this workbook entitled *Applications for Personal Discipleship* and *Personal or Family Needs* (pages 107–109). Once completed, you may want to tear out these sheets for easier reference when completing future quiet time sections. Remember to check off the appropriate diamond next to each discipline of prayer as you complete it during your daily quiet time with God.

Quiet Times for Weeks Nine and Ten

Date: _____   Passage: Psalm 116:1–2

⇒ **Remember** the disciplines of prayer (◊ praise, ◊ confession, ◊ thanksgiving, ◊ supplication).
⇒ **Request** that God speak to you from His Word.
⇒ **Read** the passage.
⇒ **Record** in the space below what God said.

⇒ **Reflect** on how this will affect your life today.

Date: _____   Passage: Isaiah 62:6–7

⇒ **Remember** the disciplines of prayer (◊ praise, ◊ confession, ◊ thanksgiving, ◊ supplication).
⇒ **Request** that God speak to you from His Word.
⇒ **Read** the passage.
⇒ **Record** in the space below what God said.

⇒ **Reflect** on how this will affect your life today.

Date: _____   Passage: Matthew 6:5–8

⇒ **Remember** the disciplines of prayer (◊ praise, ◊ confession, ◊ thanksgiving, ◊ supplication).
⇒ **Request** that God speak to you from His Word.
⇒ **Read** the passage.
⇒ **Record** in the space below what God said.

⇒ **Reflect** on how this will affect your life today.

Date: _____   Passage: Matthew 6:9–13

⇒ **Remember** the disciplines of prayer (◊ praise, ◊ confession, ◊ thanksgiving, ◊ supplication).
⇒ **Request** that God speak to you from His Word.
⇒ **Read** the passage.
⇒ **Record** in the space below what God said.

⇒ **Reflect** on how this will affect your life today.

Date: _____   Passage: Matthew 18:19–20

⇒ **Remember** the disciplines of prayer (◊ praise, ◊ confession, ◊ thanksgiving, ◊ supplication).
⇒ **Request** that God speak to you from His Word.
⇒ **Read** the passage.
⇒ **Record** in the space below what God said.

⇒ **Reflect** on how this will affect your life today.

Date: _____   Passage: Luke 22:41–42

Remember the disciplines of prayer (◊ praise, ◊ confession, ◊ thanksgiving, ◊ supplication).

⇒ **Request** that God speak to you from His Word.
⇒ **Read** the passage.
⇒ **Record** in the space below what God said.

⇒ **Reflect** on how this will affect your life today.

Date: _____   Passage: John 15:7

⇒ **Remember** the disciplines of prayer (◊ praise, ◊ confession, ◊ thanksgiving, ◊ supplication).
⇒ **Request** that God speak to you from His Word.
⇒ **Read** the passage.
⇒ **Record** in the space below what God said.

⇒ **Reflect** on how this will affect your life today.

Date: _____   Passage: John 16:23–27

⇒ **Remember** the disciplines of prayer (◊ praise, ◊ confession, ◊ thanksgiving, ◊ supplication).
⇒ **Request** that God speak to you from His Word.
⇒ **Read** the passage.
⇒ **Record** in the space below what God said.

⇒ **Reflect** on how this will affect your life today.

Date: _____   Passage: Ephesians 3:14–21

⇒ **Remember** the disciplines of prayer (◊ praise, ◊ confession, ◊ thanksgiving, ◊ supplication).

⇒ **Request** that God speak to you from His Word.

⇒ **Read** the passage.

⇒ **Record** in the space below what God said.

⇒ **Reflect** on how this will affect your life today.

Date: _____   Passage: Philippians 4:6–7, 19–20

⇒ **Remember** the disciplines of prayer (◊ praise, ◊ confession, ◊ thanksgiving, ◊ supplication).

⇒ **Request** that God speak to you from His Word.

⇒ **Read** the passage.

⇒ **Record** in the space below what God said.

⇒ **Reflect** on how this will affect your life today.

Date: _____   Passage: James 1:5–8

⇒ **Remember** the disciplines of prayer (◊ praise, ◊ confession, ◊ thanksgiving, ◊ supplication).
⇒ **Request** that God speak to you from His Word.
⇒ **Read** the passage.
⇒ **Record** in the space below what God said.

⇒ **Reflect** on how this will affect your life today.

Date: _____   Passage: James 4:1–4

⇒ **Remember** the disciplines of prayer (◊ praise, ◊ confession, ◊ thanksgiving, ◊ supplication).
⇒ **Request** that God speak to you from His Word.
⇒ **Read** the passage.
⇒ **Record** in the space below what God said.

⇒ **Reflect** on how this will affect your life today.

Date: _____   Passage: 1 John 3:21–22

⇒ **Remember** the disciplines of prayer (◊ praise, ◊ confession, ◊ thanksgiving, ◊ supplication).
⇒ **Request** that God speak to you from His Word.
⇒ **Read** the passage.
⇒ **Record** in the space below what God said.

⇒ **Reflect** on how this will affect your life today.

Date: _____   Passage: 1 John 5:14–15

⇒ **Remember** the disciplines of prayer (◊ praise, ◊ confession, ◊ thanksgiving, ◊ supplication).
⇒ **Request** that God speak to you from His Word.
⇒ **Read** the passage.
⇒ **Record** in the space below what God said.

⇒ **Reflect** on how this will affect your life today.

CHAPTER 7

Intercession

Now I urge you, brethren, by our Lord Jesus Christ and by the love of the Spirit, to strive together with me in your prayers to God for me.

—Romans 15:30

Blest be the tie that binds
Our hearts in Christian love;
The fellowship of kindred minds
Is like to that above.
Before our Father's throne
We pour our ardent prayers;
Our fears, our hopes, our aims are one,
Our comforts and our cares.

—*Blest Be the Tie That Binds*

Ever notice yourself finding it easier to ask for something on behalf someone else as opposed to making requests for you? Have you ever defended someone else's honor or position when, if the situation involved only you, you might very well let the comments pass? Do you get more upset over injustices done to your own family members than to yourself? These questions bring to light the reality that you already possess all of the motivation you need to pray for your fellow man.

Shifting from Self to Others

It may or may not have occurred to you that up until this time, your prayer requests centered predominately on yourself and your relationship with God. Now you will learn the real power of prayer, namely, the ability to serve, to minister to, to bless, to encourage, and to protect people all over the face of the earth without ever moving from the spot where you and God daily meet. Read the following passages, and note next to each verse how it reveals this power of prayer.

- Romans 15:30
- 2 Corinthians 1:11
- Philemon 1:22
- Ephesians 6:18–19

Reflecting on these passages, choose a verse that best expresses your feelings in this area, and circle the verse. Now turn to the Convictions in Prayer page of this workbook (page 106). Under *Type of Prayer* and *Scripture Reference* in space number five, write *Intercession* followed by the previously selected verse that spoke the most clearly to you on this issue. Then in the space provided underneath these headings, write out the verse in its entirety. Now when satan challenges you when you ask God for something for others, you possess an answer with which to silence him.

A Global Labor

Consider what situation or ministry setting you view as your *ministry fantasy*. Perhaps it involves going to a country on the opposite side of the world or ministering to a specific people group. Maybe you would like to start a seminary or lead evangelistic crusades. If you have never considered a *ministry wish*, spend a few moments doing so now. In the space below list the area(s) in which you think it would be exciting for God to call you into full-time ministry.

The following quiet times focus on the power of intercessory prayers. You will discover that, even if God never calls you to the mission field, you still labor in foreign fields through prayer. Even if God never calls you into student work, to abortion protests, to inner-city outreach, to translate the Scriptures into new languages, or to mass evangelism, you still labor alongside such ministries through prayer.

Before beginning the daily quiet times alone with God for this chapter, complete the worksheets entitled *Family and Friends*, *Ministry Fantasies*, and *Unbelievers* (pages 111-115). Once completed, you may want to tear out these sheets for easier reference when completing future quiet time sections. Remember to check off the appropriate diamond next to each discipline of prayer as you complete it during your daily quiet time with God.

QUIET TIMES FOR WEEKS
ELEVEN AND TWELVE

Date: _____   Passage: 1 Samuel 12:23

⇒ **Remember** the disciplines of prayer (◊ praise, ◊ confession, ◊ thanksgiving, ◊ supplication, ◊ intercession).

⇒ **Request** that God speak to you from His Word.

⇒ **Read** the passage.

⇒ **Record** in the space below what God said.

⇒ **Reflect** on how this will affect your life today.

_____

Date: _____   Passage: Job 1:1–5

⇒ **Remember** the disciplines of prayer (◊ praise, ◊ confession, ◊ thanksgiving, ◊ supplication, ◊ intercession).

⇒ **Request** that God speak to you from His Word.

⇒ **Read** the passage.

⇒ **Record** in the space below what God said.

⇒ **Reflect** on how this will affect your life today.

Date: _____   Passage: Matthew 5:44

⇒ **Remember** the disciplines of prayer (◊ praise, ◊ confession, ◊ thanksgiving, ◊ supplication, ◊ intercession).
⇒ **Request** that God speak to you from His Word.
⇒ **Read** the passage.
⇒ **Record** in the space below what God said.

⇒ **Reflect** on how this will affect your life today.

Date: _____   Passage: Luke 23:33–34

⇒ **Remember** the disciplines of prayer (◊ praise, ◊ confession, ◊ thanksgiving, ◊ supplication, ◊ intercession).
⇒ **Request** that God speak to you from His Word.
⇒ **Read** the passage.
⇒ **Record** in the space below what God said.

⇒ **Reflect** on how this will affect your life today.

Date: _____   Passage: John 17:9–26

⇒ **Remember** the disciplines of prayer (◊ praise, ◊ confession, ◊ thanksgiving, ◊ supplication, ◊ intercession).
⇒ **Request** that God speak to you from His Word.
⇒ **Read** the passage.
⇒ **Record** in the space below what God said.

⇒ **Reflect** on how this will affect your life today.

Date: _____   Passage: Romans 10:1

⇒ **Remember** the disciplines of prayer (◊ praise, ◊ confession, ◊ thanksgiving, ◊ supplication, ◊ intercession).
⇒ **Request** that God speak to you from His Word.
⇒ **Read** the passage.
⇒ **Record** in the space below what God said.

⇒ **Reflect** on how this will affect your life today.

Date: _____   Passage: Romans 15:30

⇒ **Remember** the disciplines of prayer (◊ praise, ◊ confession, ◊ thanksgiving, ◊ supplication, ◊ intercession).
⇒ **Request** that God speak to you from His Word.
⇒ **Read** the passage.
⇒ **Record** in the space below what God said.

⇒ **Reflect** on how this will affect your life today.

Date: _____   Passage: 2 Corinthians 1:11

⇒ **Remember** the disciplines of prayer (◊ praise, ◊ confession, ◊ thanksgiving, ◊ supplication, ◊ intercession).
⇒ **Request** that God speak to you from His Word.
⇒ **Read** the passage.
⇒ **Record** in the space below what God said.

⇒ **Reflect** on how this will affect your life today.

Date: _____   Passage: Ephesians 6:18–20

⇒ **Remember** the disciplines of prayer (◊ praise, ◊ confession, ◊ thanksgiving, ◊ supplication, ◊ intercession).
⇒ **Request** that God speak to you from His Word.
⇒ **Read** the passage.
⇒ **Record** in the space below what God said.

⇒ **Reflect** on how this will affect your life today.

Date: _____   Passage: Colossians 1:9–12

⇒ **Remember** the disciplines of prayer (◊ praise, ◊ confession, ◊ thanksgiving, ◊ supplication, ◊ intercession).
⇒ **Request** that God speak to you from His Word.
⇒ **Read** the passage.
⇒ **Record** in the space below what God said.

⇒ **Reflect** on how this will affect your life today.

Date: _____   Passage: Colossians 4:12–13

⇒ **Remember** the disciplines of prayer (◊ praise, ◊ confession, ◊ thanksgiving, ◊ supplication, ◊ intercession).
⇒ **Request** that God speak to you from His Word.
⇒ **Read** the passage.
⇒ **Record** in the space below what God said.

⇒ **Reflect** on how this will affect your life today.

Date: _____   Passage: 2 Thessalonians 1:11–12

⇒ **Remember** the disciplines of prayer (◊ praise, ◊ confession, ◊ thanksgiving, ◊ supplication, ◊ intercession).
⇒ **Request** that God speak to you from His Word.
⇒ **Read** the passage.
⇒ **Record** in the space below what God said.

⇒ **Reflect** on how this will affect your life today.

Date: _____   Passage: 2 Thessalonians 3:1

⇒ **Remember** the disciplines of prayer (◊ praise, ◊ confession, ◊ thanksgiving, ◊ supplication, ◊ intercession).
⇒ **Request** that God speak to you from His Word.
⇒ **Read** the passage.
⇒ **Record** in the space below what God said.

⇒ **Reflect** on how this will affect your life today.

Date: _____   Passage: James 5:14–18

⇒ **Remember** the disciplines of prayer (◊ praise, ◊ confession, ◊ thanksgiving, ◊ supplication, ◊ intercession).
⇒ **Request** that God speak to you from His Word.
⇒ **Read** the passage.
⇒ **Record** in the space below what God said.

⇒ **Reflect** on how this will affect your life today.

CHAPTER 8

Spiritual Warfare

Be of sober spirit, be on the alert. Your adversary, the devil,
prowls around like a roaring lion, seeking someone to devour.
But resist him, firm in your faith, knowing that the same experiences of
suffering are being accomplished by your brethren who are in the world.

—1 Peter 5:8–9

Did we in our own strength confide, our striving would be losing,
Were not the right man on our side, the man of God's own choosing.
Dost ask who that may be? Christ Jesus, it is He –
Lord Sabaoth His name, from age to age the same,
And He must win the battle.

—A Mighty Fortress is Our God

Can you recall a time when you really needed help and someone dependable bailed you out? Perhaps your father, spouse, or friend jumped into action on your behalf. Regardless of the person's relationship to you, you did not hesitate to ask, and they did not waste time in responding. This is the essence of spiritual warfare. During your quiet times alone with God, opportunities abound for you to join in the spiritual struggle going on all around you.

Engaging the Conflict

This last area of prayer is a crucial, yet often neglected, discipline. It is our spiritual tool by which we combat a very real, though unseen, enemy. Read the following verses carefully, and write out the main idea of each passage in the space provided below.

- Psalm 89:22–23

- Romans 16:20

- Hebrew 2:12–16

- James 4:7

- 1 John 4:1–4

- 1 John 5:4–6, 18–20

- Revelation 12:10–11

- Revelation 20:7–10

Reflecting on these passages, choose a verse that best expresses your feelings in this area, and circle the verse. Now turn to the Convictions in Prayer page of this workbook (page 106). Under *Type of Prayer* and *Scripture Reference* in space number six, write *Spiritual Warfare* followed by the previously selected verse that spoke the most clearly to you on this issue. Then in the space provided underneath these headings, write out the verse in its entirety. Now when satan tempts you not to pray against him, you will have an answer with which to quiet him.

Marching Onward

Both satan and his demonic kingdom are real, but even more real is the power of the shed blood of Christ, the witness of the Spirit within you, the authority and rule of your sovereign God and Father over His kingdom, and the myriad of elect angels under His service. God's kingdom wages war against the rebellious kingdom of satan. From now on your prayers will strike a blow at satan and his pitiful, evil attempts at thwarting the ever-forward march of the armies of the living God. Before beginning the daily quiet times alone with God for this chapter, complete the worksheet entitled *Victory in Spiritual Warfare* (see page 117). Once completed, you may want to tear out this sheet for easier reference when completing future quiet time sections.

You are now making use of all the major aspects of prayer. A helpful acronym by which to remember these disciplines of prayer is *ACTSIS*:

- ⇒ **Adoration**
- ⇒ **Confession**
- ⇒ **Thanksgiving**
- ⇒ **Supplication**
- ⇒ **Intercession**
- ⇒ **Spiritual Warfare**

Remember to check off the appropriate diamond next to each discipline of prayer as you complete it during your daily quiet time with God.

Quiet Times for Weeks Thirteen and Fourteen

Date: _____   Passage: John 12:30–33

⇒ **Remember** the disciplines of prayer (◊ praise, ◊ confession, ◊ thanksgiving, ◊ supplication, ◊ intercession, ◊ spiritual warfare).
⇒ **Request** that God speak to you from His Word.
⇒ **Read** the passage.
⇒ **Record** in the space below what God said.

⇒ **Reflect** on how this will affect your life today.

___

Date: _____   Passage: John 17:15

⇒ **Remember** the disciplines of prayer (◊ praise, ◊ confession, ◊ thanksgiving, ◊ supplication, ◊ intercession, ◊ spiritual warfare).
⇒ **Request** that God speak to you from His Word.
⇒ **Read** the passage.
⇒ **Record** in the space below what God said.

⇒ **Reflect** on how this will affect your life today.

Date: _____   Passage: Acts 26:18

⇒ **Remember** the disciplines of prayer (◊ praise, ◊ confession, ◊ thanksgiving, ◊ supplication, ◊ intercession, ◊ spiritual warfare).
⇒ **Request** that God speak to you from His Word.
⇒ **Read** the passage.
⇒ **Record** in the space below what God said.

⇒ **Reflect** on how this will affect your life today.

Date: _____   Passage: Colossians 1:13–14

⇒ **Remember** the disciplines of prayer (◊ praise, ◊ confession, ◊ thanksgiving, ◊ supplication, ◊ intercession, ◊ spiritual warfare).
⇒ **Request** that God speak to you from His Word.
⇒ **Read** the passage.
⇒ **Record** in the space below what God said.

⇒ **Reflect** on how this will affect your life today.

Date: _____   Passage: Colossians 2:13–15

⇒ **Remember** the disciplines of prayer (◊ praise, ◊ confession, ◊ thanksgiving, ◊ supplication, ◊ intercession, ◊ spiritual warfare).
⇒ **Request** that God speak to you from His Word.
⇒ **Read** the passage.
⇒ **Record** in the space below what God said.

⇒ **Reflect** on how this will affect your life today.

Date: _____   Passage: Hebrews 2:14–18

⇒ **Remember** the disciplines of prayer (◊ praise, ◊ confession, ◊ thanksgiving, ◊ supplication, ◊ intercession, ◊ spiritual warfare).
⇒ **Request** that God speak to you from His Word.
⇒ **Read** the passage.
⇒ **Record** in the space below what God said.

⇒ **Reflect** on how this will affect your life today.

Date: _____   Passage: James 4:7

⇒ **Remember** the disciplines of prayer (◊ praise, ◊ confession, ◊ thanksgiving, ◊ supplication, ◊ intercession, ◊ spiritual warfare).
⇒ **Request** that God speak to you from His Word.
⇒ **Read** the passage.
⇒ **Record** in the space below what God said.

⇒ **Reflect** on how this will affect your life today.

Date: _____   Passage: 1 Peter 5:8–10

⇒ **Remember** the disciplines of prayer (◊ praise, ◊ confession, ◊ thanksgiving, ◊ supplication, ◊ intercession, ◊ spiritual warfare).
⇒ **Request** that God speak to you from His Word.
⇒ **Read** the passage.
⇒ **Record** in the space below what God said.

⇒ **Reflect** on how this will affect your life today.

Date: _____   Passage: 1 John 2:12–14

⇒ **Remember** the disciplines of prayer (◊ praise, ◊ confession, ◊ thanksgiving, ◊ supplication, ◊ intercession, ◊ spiritual warfare).
⇒ **Request** that God speak to you from His Word.
⇒ **Read** the passage.
⇒ **Record** in the space below what God said.

⇒ **Reflect** on how this will affect your life today.

Date: _____   Passage: 1 John 3:7–8

⇒ **Remember** the disciplines of prayer (◊ praise, ◊ confession, ◊ thanksgiving, ◊ supplication, ◊ intercession, ◊ spiritual warfare).
⇒ **Request** that God speak to you from His Word.
⇒ **Read** the passage.
⇒ **Record** in the space below what God said.

⇒ **Reflect** on how this will affect your life today.

Date: _____   Passage: 1 John 5:4–6

⇒ **Remember** the disciplines of prayer (◊ praise, ◊ confession, ◊ thanksgiving, ◊ supplication, ◊ intercession, ◊ spiritual warfare).
⇒ **Request** that God speak to you from His Word.
⇒ **Read** the passage.
⇒ **Record** in the space below what God said.

⇒ **Reflect** on how this will affect your life today.

Date: _____   Passage: 1 John 5:18–20

⇒ **Remember** the disciplines of prayer (◊ praise, ◊ confession, ◊ thanksgiving, ◊ supplication, ◊ intercession, ◊ spiritual warfare).
⇒ **Request** that God speak to you from His Word.
⇒ **Read** the passage.
⇒ **Record** in the space below what God said.

⇒ **Reflect** on how this will affect your life today.

Date: _____   Passage: Revelation 12:10–11

⇒ **Remember** the disciplines of prayer (◊ praise, ◊ confession, ◊ thanksgiving, ◊ supplication, ◊ intercession, ◊ spiritual warfare).
⇒ **Request** that God speak to you from His Word.
⇒ **Read** the passage.
⇒ **Record** in the space below what God said.

⇒ **Reflect** on how this will affect your life today.

Date: _____   Passage: Revelation 20:17–20

⇒ **Remember** the disciplines of prayer (◊ praise, ◊ confession, ◊ thanksgiving, ◊ supplication, ◊ intercession, ◊ spiritual warfare).
⇒ **Request** that God speak to you from His Word.
⇒ **Read** the passage.
⇒ **Record** in the space below what God said.

⇒ **Reflect** on how this will affect your life today.

MOVING FORWARD

CHAPTER 9

From Project to Lifestyle

Devote yourselves to prayer,
keeping alert in it with an attitude of thanksgiving.

—Colossians 4:2

I need Thee every hour, most gracious Lord;
No tender voice like Thine can peace afford.
I need Thee, O I need Thee; every hour I need Thee!
O bless me now, my Savior, I come to Thee.

—*I Need Thee Every Hour*

Many relationships begin with a *project*. Perhaps a business or school task brings you together. Maybe you go on a blind date for the sake of a friend, or you find yourself thrown together by virtue of sharing a church responsibility. Whatever the case, most relationships begin within the framework of a planned activity.

Familiarity in Prayer

When preparing to spend time with a new acquaintance, you probably think something to the effect of, *What will we do? What will we talk about? How do I fill up the time?* But the more time you spend with that individual and the more effort you exert in building the relationship, the less formal your times become. Before long you just get together. True, there is structure, but it is no longer the centerpiece of the relationship; now the relationship itself comprises the centerpiece, and any structure exists merely as a help. In the same way, the more devoted time you give to prayer, the less formal structure you will find yourself needing to spend daily time with God and in His Word. Read the verses below, and write out a brief summary beside each passage describing how it encourages you to persevere in daily time in prayer.

- Genesis 32:24–26
- Nehemiah 1:1–11
- Luke 18:1–8
- James 5:16–18

Building on the Foundation

As you grow more comfortable in your daily time in prayer with God, you will, of course, want to continue to utilize the six basic disciplines of prayer, since God's Word teaches you to use these aspects of prayer in your relationship with Him. Just as after years of marriage, a good husband still practices those social skills which he cultivated during courtship, so, too, you must not forget what formed the foundation of your daily time with God. However, in the same way that the wise husband learns what pleases his wife and begins to build events around those items without needing to review each detail with her ahead of time, you also will grow out of your dependence on workbooks (such as this one) to guide your time in prayer as you discover your particular devotional and worship style.

Before developing your own prayer notebook, take a few moments to review the disciplines of prayer that you have studied thus far. In the spaces provided list the six basic disciplines of prayer, and write a short description of each *without* referring back to your notebook.

1) _____ :

2) _____ :

3) _____ :

4) _____ :

5) _____ :

6) _____ :

Now you are ready to develop a Prayer Notebook of your very own. The following chapter provides detailed instructions on building your notebook, as well as a suggested secondary activity to facilitate the transition of moving daily times with God in prayer from project to lifestyle.

CHAPTER 10

Developing a Personal Prayer Notebook

In the morning, O Lord, You will hear my voice;
in the morning I will order my prayer to You and eagerly watch.

—Psalm 5:3

Early let us seek Thy favor; early let us seek Thy will;
Blessed Lord and only Savior, with Thy love our beings fill:
Blessed Jesus, blessed Jesus, Thou hast loved us, love us still;
Blessed Jesus, blessed Jesus, Thou hast loved us, love us still.

—Savior, Like a Shepherd Lead Us

Congratulations! After weeks of applying yourself to learning how to pray, you are ready to launch out on your own. This final chapter focuses on helping you grow as a disciple of Christ through the development of an individualized prayer notebook.

Necessary Supplies

You need only a few basic items in order to assemble your prayer notebook:

- three ring binder
- hole puncher
- blank notebook paper
- *Lord, Teach Us to Pray* workbook
- Bible
- pen or pencil.

With these elements in hand you can turn your prayer notebook into one of the most powerful tools at your disposal, both in your walk with God and in your ministry.

Assembling the Notebook

Open the *Lord, Teach Us to Pray* workbook, remove the cover sheet and Convictions in Prayer page, hole-punch these sheets, and place them at the front of the three ring binder (Prayer Notebook). Remove the blank Adoration, Confession, Thanksgiving, Supplication, Intercession, and Spiritual Warfare sheets from the workbook (pages 121-131), hole-punch these sheets, and place them next in your Prayer Notebook. These sheets now comprise the section headers for the six disciplines of prayer in your Prayer Notebook. Include within these sections any projects you found helpful during the course of your prayer study by removing those pages from the workbook and placing each sheet after its appropriate section header in your Prayer Notebook. Finally, place the blank pieces of notebook paper in your Prayer Notebook. Your finished Prayer Notebook should consist of nine basic elements:

- *Lord, Teach Us to Pray* cover sheet
- Convictions in Prayer page
- Adoration section

- Confession section
- Thanksgiving section
- Supplication section
- Intercession section
- Spiritual Warfare section
- Journal of Meditations from Scripture (use the blank notebook pages here to record your reflections from your daily time in the Word).

A Journey through the Psalms

The *Lord, Teach Us to Pray* workbook provides daily Scripture meditations to aid you in understanding God's will concerning prayer. In order to continue this process of growth in prayer, I strongly suggest that your initial meditations be taken from the book of Psalms. Since each psalm differs in length, feel free to read as many (or few) as you desire on any given day. There is no right or wrong number to read, so you are free to move at whatever pace the Holy Spirit leads you; one day it may be one psalm, another day five, and still another day you may only read a paragraph or part of a psalm.

As you read through the book of Psalms, categorize each psalm as primarily Adoration and Thanksgiving (A/T), Confession (C), Supplication (S), Intercession (I), or Spiritual Warfare (SW). As you decide on a category for each psalm, mark it in your Bible, and then record its reference on the appropriate section headers in your prayer notebook. Under the *devotional thoughts* subheadings on these pages you can keep track of any other suggestions concerning the development of your prayer notebook and walk with God. Because there are many types of psalms, do not be alarmed if some psalms do not fit into one of these six disciplines of prayer; some psalms are historical in nature, while others are centered on teaching. Also, you will find that some psalms are a combination of the different types, such that you may want to break them up among sections.

At the end of this additional study, you will have a prayer notebook that not only guides you in your prayers but also consists of prayers and passages supplied by God to you through a study of His Word. I review these section header passages when my heart is cold with regard to any discipline of prayer in order to give me a spiritual jolt—like jumper cables on an engine with a run-down battery. Whenever I find myself spiritually cold or without juice, I turn to these psalms and devotional thoughts to guide my prayers.

Final Steps

You are now ready to embark on an exciting adventure. From this point on, personalize and develop your Prayer Notebook as the Holy Spirit leads you. Just remember to follow the general set-up provided in this workbook. Begin each day by praying through the six disciplines of prayer and asking God to speak to you from His Word. Read a chapter or passage from the Bible, recording what God says to you and thanking Him for engaging with you through His Word. Lastly, go out into the world confident that you met with God and that He spoke personally to you.

Please keep in mind that while God does provide the principles found in the ACTSIS system of prayer, the application of this prayer is up to you. Enjoy your new-found spiritual maturity. I know that the Lord most certainly will.

APPENDIX

CONVICTIONS IN PRAYER

1. Type of Prayer: Scripture Reference:
   In the space below write out the entire passage for future reference.

2. Type of Prayer: Scripture Reference:
   In the space below write out the entire passage for future reference.

3. Type of Prayer: Scripture Reference:
   In the space below write out the entire passage for future reference.

4. Type of Prayer: Scripture Reference:
   In the space below write out the entire passage for future reference.

5. Type of Prayer: Scripture Reference:

In the space below write out the entire passage for future reference.

6. Type of Prayer: Scripture Reference:

In the space below write out the entire passage for future reference.

Applications for Personal Discipleship

In the spaces below write out your prayer requests as they have to do with your need to grow as a disciple. Wherever possible, include Bible verses along with the request.

The Bible

Prayer

Church Fellowship

Sharing Christ with Others

PERSONAL OR FAMILY NEEDS

In the spaces below write down your prayer requests according to the subheadings provided. Use the additional space provided at the bottom or back or this sheet to develop your own subheadings, if desired.

Relationship with Family

School/Career

Character/Personal Purity

Health/Emotional Wellness

Financial/Physical Needs

Family and Friends

In the spaces below, write down your prayer requests according to the subheadings provided. Use the additional space provided at the bottom of this sheet to develop your own subheadings, if desired.

Immediate Family

Extended Family

Friends

MINISTRY FANTASIES

In the space below begin to minister to those individuals, organizations, or people groups on your *ministry fantasy list*. Because of the awesome power of intercession, ministering in these areas is no longer a fantasy. Collect as many prayer letters, requests, and facts available to you about these ministries in which you now participate, and record each one as a prayer request. Correspond with your colaborers, keeping track of answers to prayers, as well as new requests.

Unbelievers

One important area overlooked by many individuals when praying for others is the arena of non-Christian friends and associates. You probably possess many different spheres of influence, or relationship groups in which you move, among whom you have the opportunity (through casual conversation) to influence others. Some of these may be untapped in terms of leading others to Christ. In the spaces below write down individuals' names according to the subheadings provided. Use the additional space provided at the bottom or back of this sheet to develop your own subheadings, if desired.

Family/Friends

School/Workplace

Neighborhood

Places of Business (grocery store, post office, etc.)

Professional Organizations/Clubs

VICTORY IN SPIRITUAL WARFARE

The boxes below contain a series of Bible verses to claim in satan's defeat. These are followed by evil works which satan carries out as revealed by Scripture. Read through the passages of Scripture, and select seven that jump out as especially meaningful to you. Write one of these verses under the *Victory Passage* subheading in each box. From now on when you pray, claim these victory passages as you specifically oppose satan's evil works.

Victory Passages

Matt. 16:18	Luke 1:71	John 8:12	John 12:20–33
John 16:8–11	John 17:15	Acts 26:18	Rom. 8:37–38
1 Cor. 15:54–58	2 Cor. 2:14–16	Eph. 4:8	Col. 1:13–14
Col. 2:13–15	Heb. 2:12–16	James 4:7	1 Pet. 5:9
1 John 2:12–14	1 John 3:7–8	1 John 4:1–4	1 John 5:4–6
1 John 5:18–20	Jude 1:9	Rev. 12:10–11	Rev. 20:7–10

Monday

Victory Passage:

Evil Works:

1. Murdering and lying (John 8:44)
2. Fear and destruction (1 Peter 5:8)
3. Deception and distortion (Colossians 2:8)

Tuesday

Victory Passage:

Evil Works:

1. Impersonation of the works and ministry of angels and God (2 Corinthians 11:13–15)
2. Captivating through fear (Hebrews 2:14-15)

Wednesday

Victory Passage:

Evil Works:

1. Thwarting the mission and works of God's ministers (1 Thessalonians 2:18)
2. Temptations to sin (Mark 1:13)
3. Greed and lying among Christians (Acts 5:3)

Thursday

Victory Passage:

Evil Works:

1. Illness, physical loss, depression, and discouragement (Job 1:9–11, 2:4–7)
2. Accusations (Revelation 12:10)

Friday

Victory Passage:

Evil Works:

1. Blinding to spiritual truths (2 Corinthians 4:4)
2. Tempting to worldliness (Luke 4:5–8)
3. Scheming to oppose the works of God (Ephesians 6:11)

Saturday

Victory Passage:

Evil Works:

1. Waging war on the people of God (Ephesians 6:12–13)
2. Hurling flaming arrows (Ephesians 6:16)
3. The touch, power, and idolatrous influence exerted by satan (1 John 5:18–21)

Sunday

Victory Passage:

Evil Works:

1. Snatching away the sown Word of God (Mark 4:14–15)
2. Interference with spiritual messengers (Daniel 10:12–13)
3. Opposition via satan's power over this world (1 John 5:19)

ADORATION

Psalms or Other Scripture

Devotional Thoughts

CONFESSION

Psalms or Other Scripture

Devotional Thoughts

THANKSGIVING

Psalms or Other Scripture

Devotional Thoughts

SUPPLICATION

Psalms or Other Scripture

Devotional Thoughts

INTERCESSION

Psalms or Other Scripture

Devotional Thoughts

SPIRITUAL WARFARE

Psalms or Other Scripture

Devotional Thoughts

THE PRAYER HAND ILLUSTRATION

Through prayer you daily take up your shield of faith and enter into battle in the spiritual realm. Below is an outline describing the necessity and characteristics of this *shield of faith* followed by a description of how the six disciplines of prayer can be used to take up the shield of faith.

I.   Existence of the Shield of Faith
    a.   There are weapons available to fight spiritual battles. 2 Corinthians 6:7
    b.   The shield of faith is part of this armor. Psalm 84:8–9; Ephesians 6:16

II. Characteristics of the Shield of Faith
    a.   This shield is not necessarily a defensive weapon. Job 15:26; Psalm 76:3
    b.   This shield is designed for proactive use. Psalm 35:2; Ephesians 6:13, 16
    c.   There is one (and only one) shield. Jeremiah 7:9–10
    d.   Embracing false shields results in casualties of war. 2 Kings 17:33, 18:12

III. Grasping the Shield of Faith through Prayer
    a.   Pointer finger – Adoration is the worship of God without reference to man. Psalm 95:6; Philippians 4:4
    b.   Middle finger – Confession deals with our ability to fellowship with God, not our relationship with Him. Psalm 32:5–6, 51:1
    c.   Ring finger – Thanksgiving centers not around the fact that we have it but that God would give it. Psalm 140:13; 1 Thessalonians 5:17–18
    d.   Little finger – Supplication/Intercession is a time to focus on ourselves and others. Psalm 116:1–2; Ephesians 6:18
    e.   Thumb – Spiritual Warfare is a time to remember that we and satan are not on speaking terms. James 4:7; 1 John 4:4
    f.   Palm – Application reminds us that prayer is about more than health, jobs, and relationships. Colossians 4:2; 1 Timothy 2:8

Practicing each discipline of prayer is essential to the ability to grasp and use the shield of faith. Just as the removal of a finger would hinder your ability to hold steadfastly to a shield in battle so does ignoring or forsaking even one discipline severely compromise your ability to effectively wield your own weapon of righteousness – the shield of faith.

ADDITIONAL RESOURCES

For additional resources to assist you in your daily quiet time alone with God, visit the Grace Community International webpage at www.gciweb.org. To listen to Rev. Mahon speak on the value of the daily quiet time alone with God visit the Grace Community International Sermonaudio webpage at www.sermonaudio.com/gci.